to Healing

From *Forgiveness* to Healing

Preparing Our Hearts for
the Sacrament of Reconciliation

Eric Jensen, S.J.

NOVALIS

© 2022 Novalis Publishing Inc.

Cover design and layout: Audrey Wells
Cover image: iStock

Published by Novalis

Publishing Office
1 Eglinton Avenue East, Suite 800
Toronto, Ontario, Canada
M4P 3A1

Head Office
4475 Frontenac Street
Montréal, Québec, Canada
H2H 2S2

en.novalis.ca

Cataloguing in Publication is available from Library
and Archives Canada

ISBN: 978-2-89688-838-2

Printed in Canada.

Unless otherwise noted, the Scripture quotations contained herein are
from the New Revised Standard Version of the Bible, copyrighted 1989
by the Division of Christian Education of the National Council of the
Churches of Christ in the United States of America, and are used by
permission. All rights reserved.

All rights reserved. No part of this publication may be reproduced,
stored in a retrieval system, or transmitted in any form, or by any
means, electronic, mechanical, photocopying, recording, or otherwise,
without the written permission of the publisher.

We acknowledge the support of the Government of Canada.

5   4   3   2   1   26   25   24   23   22

In Gratitude
for fifty years of friendship
with the Community of Madonna House
in Combermere, Ontario

Contents

Introduction: My Experience of Hearing Confessions – Was Something Missing? 9

I   Healing Our Wounded Trust: A Word from the Depths of Consciousness 15

II   Forgiveness and Healing: Encountering God in the Sacrament ... 21

III   Examination of Consciousness (1): What Am I Doing When I Do That? ... 27

IV   Examination of Consciousness (2): Healing Our False Judgments of Self ... 33

V   Examination of Consciousness (3): Healing Our Image of God 37

Conclusion: Renewing the Sacrament of Reconciliation 43

Appendix: A Guided Meditation
on Forgiveness and Healing **49**

Annotated Bibliography **55**

Introduction

My Experience of Hearing Confessions – Was Something Missing?

As a priest in parish ministry for sixteen years, it seemed to me that something was missing in the celebration of the sacrament of Reconciliation. Even with the help of communal penance services in Advent and Lent, I was dissatisfied with the traditional forms of the examination of conscience: they did not seem to go very deep. Looking for our sinful acts, it struck me, was a little like looking for dead or diseased leaves on a tree, and coming to confession with a list of sins – often the same ones over and over again – was like coming with a handful of dead leaves.

Staying with this image, I saw that leaves are connected to branches, that the branches are connected to a trunk, and that the trunk has roots, sometimes partly exposed above ground, but mostly buried deep beneath the surface. It's in the roots, it seemed to me, that our sinfulness is to be found. It reveals itself not so much as sin but as disorder – as shame and guilt, as fear and anger – and beneath all this disorder are wounds, especially the wounds of childhood. It is our wounded hearts that cry out for healing, and what better place to seek healing than in the sacrament of Reconciliation? *The Catechism of the Catholic Church* calls it a sacrament of healing, and yet its focus seemed to be almost exclusively on the forgiveness of sins. What was missing was the healing element of the sacrament.

One day when I was making my annual retreat at Madonna House in Combermere, Ontario, a little booklet called *The Power in Penance*, by Michael Scanlan, was put into my hands by Father Bob Wild. It was about the power of the sacrament to heal as well as to forgive. It led me to look at my wounded relationship with my older sister. She had been the cause of my first spanking at the age of four: it might seem trivial, but it was this event that wounded my trust in love. I wanted to seek healing in this area of my life. That little booklet changed my way of going to confession. It also changed my way of celebrating the sacrament as a confessor.

I returned home, and shortly afterward I was invited to celebrate the Eucharist during the last ten days of a retreat for twelve young religious women who were reflecting for a whole month on the rule of their founder. The retreat was going to end on a Sunday, and I was asked on Thursday if I could come an hour earlier the next morning to hear their confessions before Mass. And so, I suggested that they might prepare for the sacrament by reflecting on the wounds of their childhood. I spoke briefly of how I had recently received some healing in my relationship with my older sister.

The next day, Friday, I heard confessions before Mass and after lunch, then again on Saturday morning and afternoon, and finally on Sunday morning. Instead of the usual brief experience, for which these twelve women had been allotted roughly five minutes each, I had spent at least forty-five minutes with every one of them – in some cases, much more than that. What they brought to the sacrament often had little to do with sin but had a lot to do with painful hurts in the past. Most were things they had never been able to share with anyone before. Some of these had to do with accidents and with fear; surprisingly, none had to do with sexual abuse. The fact that I had talked openly about my childhood with my sister led them to reflect also on their own wounded relationships and to share them in the sacrament of Reconciliation.

In some cases, the healing began during the reflection on their history in preparation for confession and was all but completed before the celebration of the sacrament. What was most conducive to the whole experience was the contemplative month that disposed them to be open to the power of the Spirit at work in their lives and gave them the courage to share freely. Silence, solitude, and prayer all contributed to getting in touch with past hurts. To make a confession and then be prayed over for both healing and forgiveness brought them much relief. I must say I was deeply moved and thoroughly persuaded of the Power in penance, the power to heal as well as forgive.

The other element that bothered me was the examination of conscience. In his *Spiritual*

Exercises, Saint Ignatius Loyola proposes two examinations of conscience: first, a particular daily *examen* (his word) to help me grow in virtue and, second, a general examination of my thoughts, words, and deeds to prepare for a general confession of my entire life. Today we have come to call this first examination the "consciousness examen" or "awareness examen." I thought it would be helpful to apply the word *consciousness* to both kinds of examination – the one in preparation for confession as well as the daily one.

English is fortunate in having two words, *conscience* and *consciousness*, to express both concepts, whereas French has only the one word, *conscience*, for both. To reflect on my conscious awareness is very different from reflecting on my moral conscience. Instead of just looking at my thoughts, words, and deeds – at the leaves on the tree, so to speak – I could go down into the roots and try to call into consciousness the wounds that are ignored and forgotten or that lie hidden just below the level of consciousness, in order to bring them to confession for healing, as I had done with that first spanking.

What I'm proposing here is a change: first, in our way of preparing for confession, and second, in our way of celebrating the sacrament. I'm not suggesting a psychotherapeutic approach, though sometimes this may be helpful, but simply a broadening of our vision so we can focus also on the things that need healing and not just on the things that need forgiveness. I'm not asking that we redefine the sacrament of Reconciliation; it's already defined as a sacrament of healing. Rather, we need to make fuller use of its potential, bringing to it our wounds as well as our sins.

I

Healing Our Wounded Trust

A Word from the Depths of Consciousness

It's often in times of silence and solitude on retreat (though also in quiet walks by water and in the woods) that wounds from the past emerge into consciousness. Sometimes it's not a wound that emerges but a word. When I was on retreat shortly after my ordination to the priesthood, I recall two words being given to me, not from God but from deep within my consciousness. The words were *trust* and *love*, and they emerged this way: "I do not trust love." I was stunned. This meant I did not trust God's love, my parents' love, my own love, or any other love!

And so, some years later, I went to the Holy Land seeking the grace of trust. I wanted to go not as a tourist but as a pilgrim, not with a camera but with my Bible, and with a minimum of clothing and money. I wanted to make myself as vulnerable as possible, so that I would be forced to trust in God's love.

A war with Lebanon was on at that time, and Israel seemed like a dangerous destination. I was afraid of stepping on a landmine or being kidnapped and tortured, and so trust in God was something I needed more than ever. The grace I sought was given gradually while I was there but given more fully in a very dramatic fashion shortly after I returned from my pilgrimage. I was staying with the Jesuit community in Montreal and had planned to pick up a train ticket for Toronto at noon on Monday. When some friends arrived from Europe, I decided to procure the ticket the following day. On Monday at noon, a bomb went off in Montreal's Central Station, killing four young visitors from France and injuring thirty-seven people.

While I was grateful to have been spared that blast, I was especially grateful for a new understanding of trust: I saw that trust is not like a sum of money in the bank that I could draw on as it was needed. I saw it as a choice. I realized that every place is dangerous – not just Israel or Lebanon, but also the city where I had grown up and gone to school. I could choose to live in fear and trembling, or I could choose to live in trust. It was a choice I had to make not just once, but every day of my life. And so now, every morning when I rise from sleep, I entrust myself and all my needs into God's hands.

In choosing to trust, I also came gradually to understand the importance that choice plays in our lives. A friend, Nicola Schaefer, who had given birth to a daughter with severe limitations, both intellectual and physical, told me that when her daughter was born, she realized she had a choice: she could choose to be miserable, or she could choose to be happy. She said she chose to be happy. I found that astounding. I wondered whether I had ever made a similar choice. I discovered that I had.

At the end of my two-year noviceship in Guelph, I had been asked to stay on for a year studying Latin and Greek while the two close friends with whom I had entered the Jesuits went on to study philosophy in Spokane, Washington. As I stood on the hill watching them being driven to the train station (we didn't travel much by air in those days), I felt abandoned, hurt. Looking back, I saw that I was at that moment faced with a choice: I could choose to be miserable, or I could choose to be happy. I chose to be miserable – not for a day or two, but for a whole year. When I got on the train a year later to go to St. Louis for studies, I was suddenly happy again.

It was only in looking back long afterward that I came to see my being miserable not as something that had been done to me but as something I had done to myself. It was the result of a choice – an unconscious choice, but a choice nonetheless – that had been brought to my awareness and had finally surfaced. Some hurts are self-inflicted; healing comes not just with the passing of time but with their coming to consciousness. Then we can make a further choice: to bring them to God in the sacrament of Reconciliation.

When people need to do something, I tell them not just to try but to choose to do it. Someone who had never been affirmed by her parents (out of their mistaken belief that this would make her prideful) once told me, "Life would be easier if I were dead." What a contradiction. And yet this statement came out of her failed relationships and her deep feelings of worthlessness. She was not suicidal, and yet she had a conscious death wish. When I said this, she agreed with me. Death seemed easier than to go on living. I suggested she pray with these words: "I have set before you life and death … Choose life" (Deuteronomy 30:19). This was something she needed to do not just once, but every day. What she devised was very creative. She took long strips of drawing paper, wrote at the top, "Today I choose life," and listed the days of the month from 1 to 31, leaving a space to sign her name after each date. Choosing can really be a matter of life or death.

II

Forgiveness and Healing

Encountering God in the Sacrament

It is as rational and responsible human beings that we reflect on our lives and become conscious of our sinfulness. But we can be sinned against as well as sinning. In reflecting on my first spanking, I saw that it was not the spanking itself (two little taps on the bum) that was wounding; it was what followed. I was crying, of course, and my mother gave me a bath in the deep laundry sink in the kitchen and wrapped me in a big white terrycloth towel. My father, my sister, and my Aunt Stella were all sitting there, and they were laughing. I could understand later that they were not really laughing *at* me, but that's how it felt at the time: I was being held up for shaming. As the water swirled down the drain in the sink, I felt like going down the drain with it.

Unlike guilt – the recognition that I have done something bad – shame seems to imply that I *am* bad. Someone once told me that, occasionally, it's as though darkness envelops her and all she can feel is that she is a bad person. When she was born, she was received with great love and tenderness. But she had been conceived when her mother thought she was beyond conceiving and was not expecting to have another child. She did not want to be pregnant, and what the child in her womb experienced was rejection, a feeling that she was bad, as she later put it.

Neurosurgeon Wilder Penfield showed that our earliest experiences, even in the womb, are recorded in the cortex of our brain – in our memories. There is a primitive level of consciousness where early childhood wounds of rejection, even in the womb, may lie buried. Though someone may need psychological help to deal with these wounds, the sacrament of Reconciliation can build on such help (grace builds on nature). It operates on a spiritual level, which goes deeper than psychology can reach and brings healing where other approaches cannot.

The sacrament of Reconciliation does not work magic, but it can work deeper and deeper healing in the wounds we take to a confessor. Openness to the power of the Holy Spirit, on the part of both the confessor and the penitent, is what allows healing to happen. Sometimes this can be a transformative experience.

The experience of being deeply listened to with empathy, and of being heard with understanding, is in itself already healing. This is why oral confession is such an important element of the sacrament of Reconciliation. It's partly why confession is now normally done in an open place, that is, in a reconciliation room or chapel, where face-to-face confession imparts a more human aspect to the priest. Canon law reminds him that he is a healer as well as a judge, a minister of divine mercy as well as divine justice. God's compassionate love, God's mercy, is what makes forgiveness happen. It's this Power – the power of God's infinite love to forgive and to heal – that's at work in the sacrament of Reconciliation.

In my ministry of directing retreats, I've discovered that most people have wounds of some kind. I've learned to listen especially to people's accounts of their childhood and their relationship with their mother and father. The untimely death of a parent is very wounding for a child. The parents' divorce can leave children, even older children, with devastating wounds. These are just two of the things I listen for and then encourage people to talk about. Talking about them is itself very healing.

At some point, if I feel people are open to it, I may suggest that they bring to the sacrament of Reconciliation the wounds they have shared with me in spiritual direction. I find that the celebration of the sacrament is often a powerful way to end a retreat. It may involve tears (mine as well as theirs). It should involve the imposition of hands on the person's head (with permission, of course), and it usually ends with a fatherly embrace, if this seems appropriate and if the person is comfortable with it.

Both they and I often feel that God is present in such a sacramental celebration: something is changed in the depth of their being. There's a new lightness, a new freedom, a new sense of hope. The past wounds and hurts remain, of course, and healing is never complete, but people go forward with new trust and a renewed faith in God and in the Church.

III

Examination of Consciousness (1)

What Am I Doing When I Do That?

The decision Nicola Schaefer made to be happy after the birth of her daughter was a fully conscious choice, whereas my decision to be miserable was an unconscious one. I knew I had been miserable, and I thought I knew why, but I was not aware that I had chosen to be miserable. I needed first to become aware, in speaking with Nicola, that there was possibly an element of freedom involved in my misery. Then I had to reflect, to look back upon my own experience to discover whether I had made a decision to be miserable and, if so, when I had made it.

Gradually, it became clear that my feelings had been the result of something I had done to myself, something I had chosen to do, and that I had most likely done it while standing on the hill watching my friends being driven off to what seemed like greener pastures.

I was reflecting on my past feelings in order to bring fully into consciousness something that was just below the level of consciousness, like the partly exposed roots of a tree. This might be called an examination of my *unconscious*. It brought me a new awareness of myself as a more or less free, complex, feeling person and exposed the immaturity of my younger self. It helped me to understand better the decision-making that is at play in our daily lives and to try to be more attentive to the *conscious* choices that I make in my waking moments.

In examining my consciousness, I need to begin by attending to my feelings and trying to name them. What am I experiencing? Naming my feelings is a first step in trying to understand what is going on. While feelings themselves are neither right nor wrong, we can do things that intensify them, and this can sometimes make our situation worse. If you have ever had the experience of getting your car stuck in snow, you may have found yourself frustrated and angry so that you began to press on the accelerator. This spun your wheels and left you stuck still deeper in the snow. I've had an even worse experience in Manitoba gumbo or mud. At the same time that my wheels were building up thick mud inside the fenders, my frustration and anger were also intensifying. I was literally stuck in my anger. It's this intensification of anger that can be sinful.

In examining my consciousness, however, I'm not looking for sins and failures but for interior movements toward God or toward self. When my anger takes over, it's in myself that I'm stuck. If I pray for help, this is a movement away from myself and a turning toward God. As novices we were taught to make an examen twice a day, focusing especially on how well we had kept the rule of silence. We even had pinned inside our cassocks a little wire frame with a set of beads that we could slide up whenever we broke a rule. We called them misery beads. To do this is to reduce the examen to a preparation for confession rather than an examination of consciousness.

It's when the examen is linked to discernment that it becomes an awareness examen – an attentive concern with what is going on in my affective consciousness. I may be filled with love, joy, peace, and other consoling feelings that all draw me closer to God and deepen my hope, my faith, my love. Or I may experience loneliness, sadness, sluggishness, and other negative feelings that make me feel desolate and far from God. In the first case, the proper response is to give thanks for the consolations. In the second case, I should do my best to act against the desolations. I would go further and say that I need to choose to act against the desolations, and to do nothing that would intensify these negative feelings. The simplest way to act against desolation is to pray for help.

Besides feelings, there are also thoughts. I need also to pay attention to what thoughts I may be dwelling on. If I'm in consolation, my thoughts will likely be positive, whereas if I'm in desolation, my thoughts will be negative. My thinking will reinforce my feelings and, while it's good to reinforce my positive feelings, I don't want to reinforce the negative ones. Again, I need to ask for God's help to substitute thinking about the good things in my life – my life itself, my faith, the people who have taught me, encouraged me, loved me, and any other graces I can name – and dwell on these rather than the others.

Ultimately, what I am doing in this sort of consciousness examen is trying to discern what God wants me to do, what God wants me to choose, so that my life itself becomes one of continuous discernment. Instead of making unconscious choices, I want to make conscious ones. Instead of making bad or foolish decisions, I want to make good ones, wise ones. And so, the examen always begins by asking for light, to see what God wants me to see and to choose what God wants me to choose. A prayer I first learned as a Jesuit novice incorporates some of this:

> O my Jesus, help me to realize that I am in your presence and that you behold me as I pray. Enlighten my mind and touch my heart, that I may know your holy will and do it gladly, for your honour and glory and for the good of my soul. Amen.

It's not only my mind that desires to know God's will; it's especially my heart. This is the gift that young Solomon begged for: "A heart to understand" (New Jerusalem Bible, 1 Kings 3:9). But, as I've said, our hearts are usually wounded and need healing to understand rightly and choose wisely.

IV

Examination of Consciousness (2)

Healing Our False Judgments of Self

Examining my consciousness, it should now be clear, is not like looking into my soul to observe something. Rather, it's about attending – about being attentive to or paying attention to my interior experience. It begins with my affective consciousness, with my feelings or bodily sensations, and moves on to consider my related thinking and the thoughts I may be dwelling on that come from my feelings.

Besides feelings and thoughts, there are also judgments. These are not the reflective judgments that help me decide the correctness or completeness of my understanding, but rather the false judgments about myself that often arise from my negative feelings. We all have a tendency to say negative things about ourselves: for instance, to call myself stupid when I make a mistake. That's a judgment that may be more or less true some of the time, but there are false judgments about ourselves that can be very damaging.

A young woman who used to see me for spiritual direction once came with her journal in which she had written, in large black letters with a big wax crayon, "I AM UGLY! NOBODY LOVES ME! I HATE MY WORK! NOTHING HAS CHANGED!" I asked to look at what she had written and, with my pen, I circled what seemed to be the key words.

"UGLY: Do you really think you're ugly?" I asked. (She was really quite beautiful.) She answered, "No."

"NOBODY loves you: Is this true? If even one person loves you, it's false."

"You HATE your work: Last month you told me there were lots of things about your work that you love."

"NOTHING has changed: It seems to me that a lot has changed since I last saw you." As it turned

Examination of Consciousness (2)

out, every one of her statements or judgments was false, but the feelings out of which they had sprung were very real and very strong, as attested to by the way she had written them down so large and black.

This was a very helpful and useful distinction to make: between what is *real* and what is *false*. "Head" people, like me, may at times be out of touch with their feelings, but when these are very strong, it's impossible to deny their existence, their reality. The judgments based on these feelings are also real – real judgments – but in this case they were not true but false judgments. To make such a distinction in the midst of all that was going on, that gave rise to both the feelings and the judgments, would be difficult if not impossible. Later, when the feelings had subsided somewhat, it might be possible to make such a distinction during the examen – possible, but still difficult. Like this young woman, we may need help. This is why a spiritual director, or a wise and trusted friend, can be of assistance.

One can also bring all this – these negative feelings and false judgments – to the sacrament of Reconciliation for healing. Here it's not a matter of confessing only my sins, like self-hatred, but of bringing my troubled and wounded heart for healing. It's my inner self, my feeling and judging self, that is experiencing confusion and is in need of a compassionate and understanding presence, and most of all, in need of the loving *Power* of the Spirit of God who is compassion and love itself.

V

Examination of Consciousness (3)

Healing Our Image of God

No one has seen God, yet most of us have seen paintings or stained-glass windows depicting God, and all of us have imaginations and memories in which are stored images of God. The Bible contains many different images of God: some frightening, some consoling. Perhaps the truest and most beautiful image is that given us by Luke in his parable of "The Father and the Two Lost Sons" (Luke 15:11-32). It has frequently been named "The Parable of the Prodigal Son," which directs our focus to the first half of the narrative. Had it been called "The Parable of the Older Brother," this would have given it a very different slant. But placing the emphasis on the Father, as does Kenneth Bailey (see the Bibliography) seems finally to name what this story is all about. It presents us with a patriarchal figure who is meant by Jesus to be a true image of God the Father.

In praying with this parable, we usually put ourselves in the place of the younger son, who asks for his inheritance in advance of his father's death. In the cultural setting of the Middle East, this would be a grave offence, a dishonourable deed, something which no son would be likely to do and with which no father would comply. But in the parable, this is exactly what the younger son does, and his father actually grants his request. A key point in the story is that the father *divided* his property between both his sons. The older brother should have refused and said he wanted no part of this shocking affair, but instead he accepts his share of the inheritance as well. The father would have given each a deed to the property, a one-third share to the younger son and two-thirds to his brother.

How did the younger one turn his deed into cash? Because the whole transaction was so dishonourable, no one in the village would have purchased it, and so the older brother must have done so. This would make sense of the father's statement that "All that is mine is yours" (Luke 15:31). When the younger son later returns to his father, having spent all he had, it's not because of any motive other than hunger: he's literally starving to death. And so, he acknowledges his sinfulness, which seems to have sprung largely from ignorance and immaturity. Only on returning does he begin to discover his father's overwhelming and unconditional love. He couldn't possibly imagine that he has done anything to earn this love – in fact, he deserves to be punished, even totally rejected. If we ask what image he earlier had of his father, it's difficult to say. Perhaps he thought him an old fool or maybe just an overindulgent parent, easily manipulated. Probably just a minor in years, this son is also a minor character in the story, hardly deserving of having the parable named for him.

The older brother, however, is altogether different. Having agreed to accept the deed to his share of the property, he has put himself in a new relationship with his father: that of a servant rather than a son. By hard work and obedience, he feels he has earned his father's love, or at least a reward. Instead, he sees his brother seemingly rewarded for shameful behaviour, yet he himself treats his father most shamefully: in refusing to go into the house, he forces his father to come outside, and then berates him in front of the guests and servants. We already know his image of the father: that of an unjust boss.

The older brother is blind to the father's love for him and to his great humility. Much as the father longs to show this son his love, he cannot, since it would only be received as a reward for hard work. The father's hands are tied, as it were. Thus, the older son finds himself in a hell of his own choosing. He remains outside, weeping and gnashing his teeth, while the father pleads with him to come in. Meanwhile, the joyful celebration continues without him. Or does it? If we ask ourselves who in this parable suffers the most, the answer is the father. The children bring all kinds of grief upon themselves, but it's their father, in his boundless compassion, who suffers with them. The feasting may go on, but the father remains sadly mindful of the one who is absent.

Both brothers are sinful, but the source of their sinfulness lies in their false images of their father. They need to be forgiven, surely, but they need most of all to be healed of their blindness and misunderstanding, of seeing their father's humility as weakness, his love as indulgence or folly. We, too, may need to be forgiven at times, but unless we are also healed of our false images of God, we go on sinning. If, however, we could begin to glimpse even a little of God's immense love for us, if we could understand something of his compassion and grasp his deep humility, there's no way we would risk offending him or think of turning our backs on him. "No cripple wouldn't creep one mile uphill to only see him smile," as e.e. cummings says in his great poem "my father moved through dooms of love."

One way we can come to better appreciate our loving, compassionate, and humble God is by contemplating his image in the parable of "The Father and the Two Lost Sons." When we begin to understand something of what needs to be healed in us – all that is twisted and distorted, all the false images and lies we may have absorbed over the years – then, like the younger son, we can turn to our God, not just for forgiveness but also for healing of all those images that have wounded our understanding. Then will our conscience be clear and our consciousness expanded to receive wholeheartedly what we most deeply long for: God's infinite love.

The parable remains unfinished, and so we must ask what the older son will do. Will he finally come to himself and, like his brother, ask to come in? This seems to be what's implied by the parable's open structure, but for this to happen, he will first have to work through his anger at his father and his hatred of his brother and admit at last that he was wrong. Because he is so convinced that he's right, this will be a long and painful process of purification – in other words, a purgatory. Otherwise, we would have to say that he remains in his own little hell, despite the father's pleading with him to come in.

Conclusion

Renewing the Sacrament of Reconciliation

It is hoped that, just by reading this little book, people may develop a new awareness, first of all, that they have wounds, big or small; second, that they can learn how to get in touch with their wounds by examining their consciousness and not just their moral conscience; and third, that they can bring both their sins and their wounds to a priest in confession and ask to be prayed over for forgiveness and healing.

The very acknowledgement that reconciliation is a sacrament of healing, and not just of forgiveness, can open us to approach this beautiful sacrament in a new way. It can free people from a superficial approach to preparing to celebrate the sacrament, and it can help them to recognize that there is indeed something to celebrate: God's open, unconditional, welcoming, healing, and forgiving love, which can, over time, change their lives. Saint Paul tells us,

> So if anyone is in Christ, there is a new creation: everything old has passed away; see, everything has become new! All this is from God, who reconciled us to himself through Christ, and has given us the ministry of reconciliation; that is, in Christ God was reconciling the world to himself, not counting their trespasses against them, and entrusting the message of reconciliation to us. (2 Corinthians 5:17-19)

God has entrusted the message and ministry of reconciliation to us, that is, to the Apostles and to the Church. In the Byzantine and Eastern Churches, the sacraments are called mysteries. They are sacred mysteries because through them the *power* of the Holy Spirit operates to bring light and love and peace, reconciling us with God, with the Church, and with one another. This is also our understanding in the Roman Church, but with a certain overlay of legalism. Unlike the Byzantine Churches, we categorize sins as venial and mortal (or grave), while they make no such distinction. We confine the power in penance to those ordained as ministerial priests, but they do not (some monks also hear confessions and give absolution). We surround this sacrament with strict laws that touch on every aspect and level of our Christian life, while the Byzantine understanding of law is very different.

With the acceptance of private, frequent confession to a priest in the Church of the West (which eventually displaced forgiveness by a bishop, granted only once, with public penance for public sin), there came also a multiplication of manuals for confessors and an exaggerated theology of sin. Devotion was often replaced by legal duties binding "under pain of mortal sin," for instance, laws regarding Sunday worship, abstinence from meat on Fridays, and fasting during Lent. Healing, though not entirely forgotten, was meant to heal the wounds inflicted on the Church by sinning. It did not appear to recognize that the individual penitent also had wounds that sometimes cried out for healing.

Following the Second Vatican Council (1962–65), there was a renewal of the sacraments. We can ask: Is there still more we can do to make a place for healing in the sacrament of Reconciliation? Perhaps priests can begin by reflecting on their own needs for healing. They, too, carry wounds. They also stand in need of confessors who will share their concerns, who will listen to their pain, and call upon the Power of the Spirit to bring healing and forgiveness. Such self-awareness can only help them grow in compassion. With the Curé d'Ars as his model, no priest should be too busy to hear someone's confession, especially if a person calls and makes an appointment to see him.

There is an educational element involved in this process, for pastors as well as people in the pews. Not only does the Church teach; she also learns. Priests need to dialogue with one another to critique their own theology and bring it in line with the pastoral needs of their people. They can also support one another during the seasons of Advent and Lent, when there is a need for more confessors. Perhaps together they can plan services specifically for both reconciliation and healing. They can also arrange to have a parish "mission" preached on healing and forgiveness, and invite a team of lay people and priests to open up the whole matter of healing sacraments and how they can be celebrated more meaningfully. This can include the anointing of the sick, which some will still see as "extreme unction" or the sacrament of the dying. In the Appendix there follows a guided meditation, which can be adapted for use in services of reconciliation, forgiveness, and healing.

Appendix

A Guided Meditation on Forgiveness and Healing
Luke 5:17-26

To begin this meditation, you might close your eyes and try to imagine the scene. The setting is Capernaum, a small town where Jesus settled, north of the Sea of Galilee. Try to imagine the sunlight, the small stone houses. Around one of these houses is a great crowd. There are all kinds of people outside, and inside they're gathered around, listening to Jesus. Try to hear what he's saying. Place yourself among them and then imagine yourself as the paralyzed person who is brought to Jesus for healing.

One day, while [Jesus] was teaching, Pharisees and teachers of the law were sitting nearby (they had come from every village of Galilee and

Judea and from Jerusalem); and the power of the Lord was with him to heal. (5:17)

Jesus is teaching the local people, but he's also being watched by a very large and hostile group of outside observers. Jesus seems to be filled with the *power* of the Holy Spirit.

Just then some men came, carrying a paralyzed man on a bed. (5:18a)

See this paralyzed person, unable to walk or perhaps even to move. Feel his longing to be healed. Put yourself in his place. You've heard that the prophet Jesus is here in the town, but you have no way of getting to him. You're totally dependent on the generosity of others. You persuade some friends to carry you.

They were trying to bring him in and lay him before Jesus; but finding no way to bring him in because of the crowd, they went up on the roof and let him down with his bed through the tiles into the middle of the crowd in front of Jesus. (5:18b-19)

You see your friends go up on the roof and make an opening. You feel yourself being lifted up on your stretcher and passed to those on the roof. No doubt you're tense and anxious, fearful that you will be dropped and injured. Then gently you're lowered inside, and suddenly you find yourself looking up into the face of Jesus. How does he regard you? What do you read in his eyes?

When he saw their faith, he said, "Friend, your sins are forgiven you." (5:20)

As you lie there paralyzed, you probably *know* that you're a sinner. Perhaps you've even seen your plight as punishment from God. You do have faith, but is it just forgiveness you want – or is it not also healing?

Then the scribes and the Pharisees began to question, "Who is this who is speaking blasphemies? Who can forgive sins but God alone?" (5:21)

One thing you *don't* want is to be caught in the middle of a controversy. You feel your anxiety return, but you calm yourself and you put your trust in Jesus.

When Jesus perceived their questionings, he answered them, "Why do you raise such questions

in your hearts? Which is easier, to say, 'Your sins are forgiven you', or to say, 'Stand up and walk'?" (5:22-23)

Your heart skips a beat! Is Jesus actually going to do what you're longing for? Is he *really* going to answer your prayers? You fix your eyes still more intently on his, and you listen breathlessly to his words.

"But so that you may know that the Son of Man has authority on earth to forgive sins"—he said to the one who was paralyzed—"I say to you, stand up and take your bed and go to your home." (5:24)

Suddenly you feel strength being poured into your muscles, and you sense your stiff limbs begin to soften. Before you know it, you're standing!

Immediately he stood up before them, took what he had been lying on, and went to his home, glorifying God. (5:25)

Forgiveness and healing! Healing and forgiveness! You find yourself flooded with joy! You want to sing! You want to dance! As you go off carrying your cot, you want to shout to everyone you see what God has done for you through Jesus!

Amazement seized all of them, and they glorified God and were filled with awe, saying, "We have seen strange things today." (5:26)

If we have been wounded by life or sinned against by others, these may be the hurts out of which our own sinfulness grows. Anger, shame, guilt, and fear are all things that can cripple us and make us less than we're meant to be. These are the kinds of things that can also cause us to harden our heart. Knowing that we can bring them to the sacrament of Reconciliation for healing and forgiveness is already the beginning of freedom.

As you sit here quietly for a few moments, perhaps listening to some peaceful music, reflect on what you've just experienced. What are you moved to bring to the sacrament of Reconciliation? Something for healing? Something for forgiveness?

Is there anything that paralyzes you? Is there anything that keeps you from forgiving others? Is there anything that prevents you at times from coming to Jesus? Ask Jesus to show you how to come to him now in all simplicity.

Annotated Bibliography

Aschenbrenner, George A., "Consciousness Examen," *Review for Religious,* 31/1 (January 1972), 14–21. A central Ignatian exercise, the examen is best understood in relationship to the discernment of spirits. It is meant to be a time of prayer and of daily renewal and growth in our Christian and religious identity.

Bailey, Kenneth E., *Poet & Peasant* and *Through Peasant Eyes: A Literary-Cultural Approach to the Parables in Luke,* Combined Edition (Grand Rapids, MI: Eerdmans, 1983). The first volume, *Poet & Peasant*, has almost fifty pages on Luke's Prodigal Son, which Bailey calls "The Parable of the Father and the Two Lost Sons."

Bradshaw, John, *Healing the Shame that Binds You* (Deerfield Beach, FL: Health Communications, 1988). There is a kind of shame that can be called healthy, Bradshaw says, but how we can be freed from the toxic shame that imprisons and cripples us is what he is concerned with here.

Catechism of the Catholic Church (Ottawa: Canadian Conference of Catholic Bishops, 1994). In Part Two, "The Celebration of the Christian Mystery," Section Two, Chapter Two, deals with the sacraments of healing: Penance and Reconciliation (Article 4), and the Anointing of the Sick (Article 5).

Ganss, George E., S.J., *The Spiritual Exercises of Saint Ignatius: A Translation and Commentary* (St. Louis, MO: Institute of Jesuit Sources, 1992). Based on the Spanish Autograph version, this translation also makes use of the Latin Vulgate text in places and provides a very helpful commentary.

Hahn, Scott, *Swear to God: The Promise and the Power of the Sacraments* (London: Darton, Longman, and Todd, 2004). Hahn deals with the sacraments as signs, mysteries, and covenants that shape our relationship with God – much of this in terms of his own personal journey.

Harris, Thomas A., M.D., *I'm OK – You're OK* (New York: Avon, 1967). In the first chapter (pp. 25–26), the author references the neurosurgeon Wilder Penfield and says, "The evidence seems to indicate that everything which has been in our conscious awareness is recorded in detail and stored in the brain and is capable of being 'played back' in the present."

Jensen, Eric, "Forgiveness and Healing: Confession in the Spiritual Exercises," *The Way*, 56/1 (January 2017), 94–101. The *Spiritual Exercises* of Ignatius Loyola do not mention healing but focus instead on unhealthy attachments. When celebrated as a sacrament of healing as well as forgiveness, confession can be a powerful remedy in overcoming the roots of unfreedom in our lives.

———, "Hell and the Image of God in the Spiritual Exercises," *The Way*, 57/3 (July 2018), 91–102. Ignatius, like most of his contemporaries, believed that hell is an actual place, a part of God's creation full of fire and designed for the punishment of those who are damned. Behind all these assumptions are seemingly contradictory images of the God of mercy, love, and compassion. This article is an attempt to renew a major part of the theology of the Exercises.

Johnson, Darrell, *Jesus the Healer* (Vancouver: Regent College Publishing, 2017). This is a collection of sermons on Jesus' healing deeds in Matthew 8–9.

McBrien, Richard P., *Catholicism: Study Edition* (Oak Grove, MN: Winston Press, 1981). An extremely useful handbook, *Catholicism* provides the widest context for understanding the Church's sacraments. Under the heading "Sacraments of Healing," McBrien says, "In its celebration of the sacrament of Penance, the Church reveals itself as the sacrament of God's mercy in the world, but also as a sinful community, still 'on the way' to the perfection of the Kingdom."

Melloni, Javier, S.J., *The Exercises of St Ignatius Loyola in the Western Tradition* (Leominster, UK: Gracewing, 2000). As well as explaining why Ignatius delayed his Holy Land pilgrimage for almost a year at Manresa (he was being instructed by his confessor with a manual of Christian spiritual practice called *A Brief Compendium of Spiritual Exercises*), Melloni sees the Exercises as a call to continuous discernment.

Orsy, Ladislas, *The Evolving Church and the Sacrament of Penance* (Denville, NJ: Dimension Books, 1978). Here a great canon lawyer looks at some key questions: how the practice of reconciling sinners evolved in the Church's history, how ideas and persons change, and how development should continue in the future. The footnotes alone are worth the price of the book.

Raya, Archbishop Joseph M., *The Face of God: Essays in Byzantine Spirituality* (McKees Rocks, PA: God with Us Publications, 1984). Former Archbishop of Akka, Haifa, Nazareth, and All Galilee, and a member of the Madonna House Community, the author calls Christianity "a mystery of life in an embrace of Love." In the sacrament of Reconciliation, he sees Christ the healer and, with Christ, "the activity of the Holy Spirit who confers joy and confidence."

Scanlan, Michael, *The Power in Penance: Confession and the Holy Spirit* (Notre Dame, IN: Ave Maria Press, 1972). A seminal booklet on healing in the sacrament of Reconciliation, its focus is on invoking the power of the Holy Spirit to help both penitents and priests in identifying and dealing with the hidden things that impede growth in union with God.

Schaefer, Nicola, *Yes! She Knows She's Here* (Toronto: Inclusion Press, 1997; first published in 1978 as *Does She Know She's There?*). When her daughter was born, Nicola was told that Catherine would never walk, talk, or feed herself. Cath now lives in her own home, with the support of caregivers and friends.

Wild, Robert A., *The Post-Charismatic Experience: The New Wave of the Spirit* (Locust Valley, NY: Living Flame Press, 1984). What the Spirit has taught us in the Charismatic movement, Wild says, is the tremendous importance of an experiential encounter with God. This is the kind of encounter to which *all* Christians are called.

Other books by Eric Jensen, SJ

A Passionate Jesus in Holy Week

This prayerful reflection on the Passion of Jesus serves as an inspiring accompaniment for Catholics during Holy Week. Author Eric Jensen, SJ, applies Ignatian spirituality to help the reader walk through Holy Week, offering commentary that highlights various dimensions of Jesus's decisions throughout the final days and hours before his crucifixion. For Jensen, Jesus is fully aware of the situation and in control of the events that unfolded from Palm Sunday to Easter Sunday.

ISBN: 978-2-89688-771-2

Ignatius Loyola and You

This engaging book looks at the six transformations of Ignatius Loyola throughout his life as a vivid example of what such transformations might mean for our own lives. Ignatius's life – from Basque adolescent to Spanish courtier, from courtier to knight, from knight to penitent, from penitent to pilgrim, from pilgrim to student, from student to founder of a new religious order, and finally to the last stages of a long mystical transformation – comes alive with Jensen's thoughtful and easy-to-read style. Throughout the book, Jensen weaves various aspects of Ignatius's life with specific elements of his Spiritual Exercises.

ISBN: 978-2-89688-450-6

Available at your local bookstore, online at **en.novalis.ca**
or call **1-800-387-7164** to order.